Learn to read

Bug in a Rug

Words by Sue Graves
Illustrations by Jan Smith

Mom gave a present to her little bug.

"Happy birthday," said Mom. She gave him a hug.

"Wow!" said Baby Bug. He dug and he dug.

First he dug up
a big green jug.

Next he dug up an old red mug.

Then he dug
up a toy pug.
Baby Bug
gave the pug
a hug.

"What is this?"
asked Baby
Bug. He gave
it a tug.

Baby Bug found
a big, soft rug!

"Where is Baby Bug?" said Mom with a shrug.

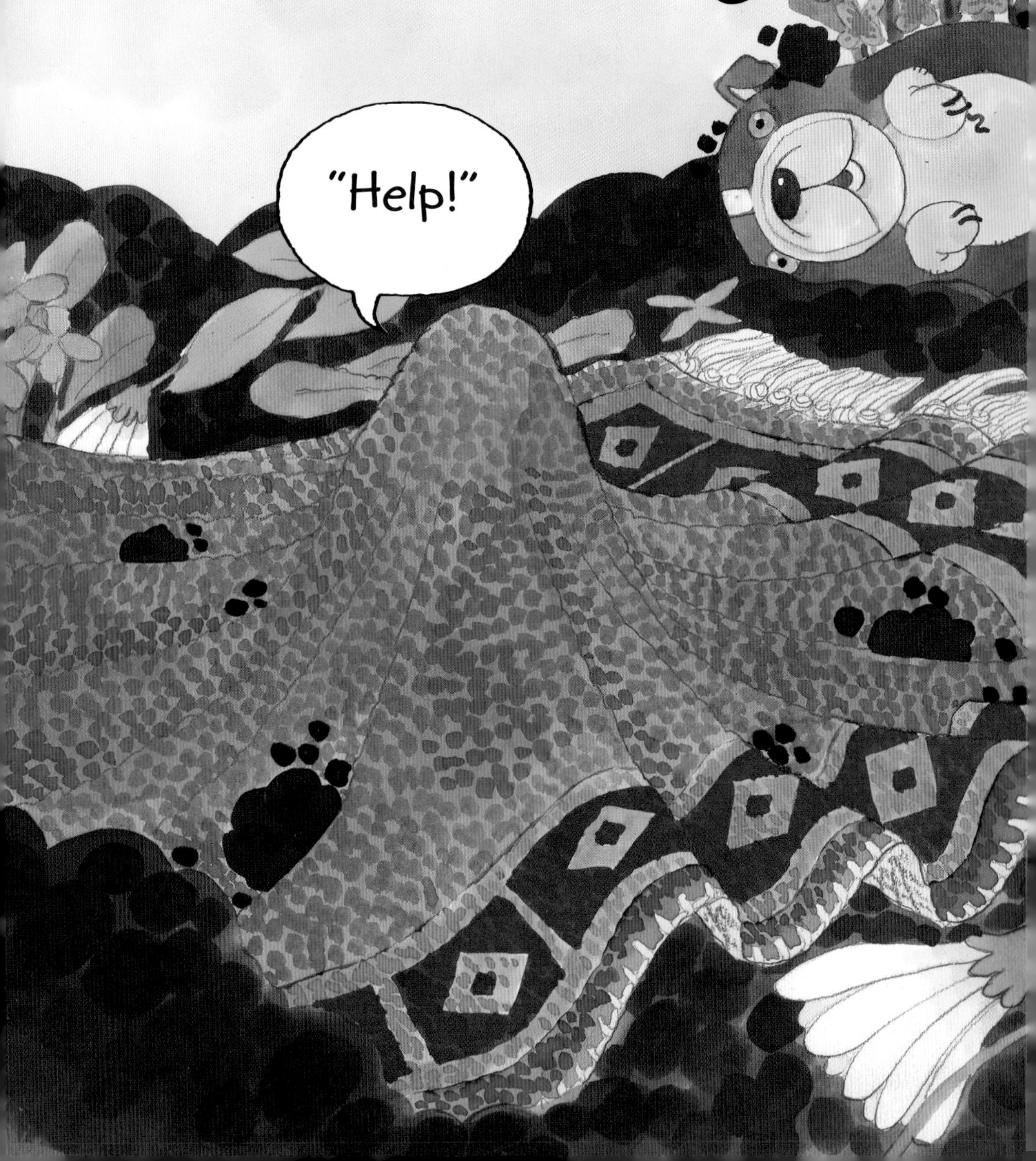

The end